CU01067319

PREFACE

As such all of us are in the search for truth, and we like, true lively lovely sweet...feelings, emotions, facts, jokes, truths...Quotes Proverbs Sayings: Please find here the Best Selective Collection of 1000 Inspiring Pleasing Thoughtful...Good Great...Pearls of Wisdom... about Life Love God.

Surendra Kapur

CHEERFUL PLEASING TRUTHS!

› "look how happy he is!" › › "he's happy because he's insane."

May you play more, laugh more, love more, live more, give more, receive more & celebrate more!

Shine your Love on others and they will blossom and bloom in your presence.

If thou wilt make a man happy, add not unto his riches but take away from his desires. ~ Epicurus

And what is a weed? A plant whose virtues have not been discovered ~ Ralph W Emerson

I feel like the grocery store has too many life decisions..

He promised me earrings, but he only pierced my ears. ~ Arabian saying

Little children, headache; big children, heartache ~
Italian Proverb

The art of medicine consists in amusing the patient
while nature cures the disease. ~ Voltaire

Life is about change. Sometimes it's beautiful,
sometimes it's painful. But most of the time, it's both.

Life doesn't need to know the right way to go
because it's going there anyway. ~ Adyashanti

We live in a wonderful world that is full of beauty,
charm, and adventure.

No matter where on this wonderful planet we live, we
can be thankful for life, love, friends ....the list is
endless.

On tops of mountains, as everywhere to hopeful
souls, it is always morning. ~ Thoreau

Be aware that you are pure consciousness. You are
not lonely or lost or abandoned. You are one with all
of Life. ~ Louise Hay

"The inner fire is the most important thing mankind
possesses." ~ Edith Sdergran

"To the mind that is still, the whole universe
surrenders." ~ Lao Tzu

The Study of Life reveals the unlimited power of the
mind, body, & spirit.

Everyday we live is a priceless gift of God, loaded with possibilities to learn something new, to gain fresh insights into His great truths.

The mind that is anxious about the future is miserable. — Seneca

"Do not fear mistakes. There are none." — Miles Davis

Stop thinking in terms of limitations and start thinking in terms of possibilities. ~ Terry Josephson

Knock the "t" off "can't". ~ George Reeves

If plan A doesn't work, the alphabet has 25 more letters.

I feel an earnest and humble desire, and shall till I die, to increase the stock of harmless cheerfulness. ~ Charles Dickens

Why in the world are we here? Surely not to live in pain and fear ~ John Lennon

Don't fight the darkness; bring in the love & light. ~ M. Ross

Faith is not the belief that God will do what you want. It is the belief that God will do what is right. ~ Max Lucado

The mind is the hurdle; it will not permit the ego to be annihilated. ~ Hazur Baba Sawan Singh

"Do not protect yourself by a fence, but rather by your friends." ~ Czech. Proverb

A friend is someone who sees through you and still enjoys the view. ~ Wilma Askinas

This is how I would die into the love I have for you: as pieces of cloud dissolve in sunlight. ~ Rumi

I have human instincts, they may be buried deep, but they're there. ~ Edward Cullen

'I love the idea of there being two sexes, don't you?' ~ James Thurber

How do you explain the things you love? You can't. You just do. ~ Dawson's Creek

When we feel love and kindness toward others, it helps us to develop inner happiness and peace. ~ Tenzin Gyatso

I have a headache but he prefers that I call him by his actual name. @Fahbins

"No change of circumstances can repair a defect of character." ~ Ralph Waldo Emerson

Housework is what a woman does that nobody notices unless she hasn't done it. ~ Evan Esar

When you're emotionally free it makes other people comfortable & happy to be around you. ~ Deepak Chopra

Don't be discouraged. It's often the last key in the bunch that opens the lock.

Things can always get better. Believe in this one simple statement and your life will mirror that!

If everyday was Christmas, life would be wonderful. People just focus on joy, peace, and love instead of problems.

Every time we love, every time we give, it's Christmas.

The oyster turns into pearl the sand which annoys it. ~ Sidney Newton Bremer

To acquire love, fill yourself up with it until you become a magnet. ~ Charles Haanel

I KNOW FOR SURE...that there are still a lot of PEOPLE out there with good hearts and kind spirits.

True wisdom comes to each of us when we realize how little we understand about life, ourselves, & the world around us. ~ Socrates

The wisest mind has something yet to learn – George Santayana

LIGHT is what we are and LOVE is how we share it.

The world does not have to change. The only thing that has to change is our attitude. ~ Gerald Jampolsky

Dear God, help me realize that I am someone wonderful. – Marianne Williamson

A genuinely happy person is one who has made others happy.

"By appreciation, we make excellence in others our own property." – Francois Voltaire

Faith is a higher faculty than reason. ~ Henry Christopher Bailey

No need for hocus pocus… just focus.

"Our life is frittered away by detail. Simplify, simplify." ~ Henry David Thoreau

NICE WISE SAYINGS...

As long as you live, keep learning how to live. ~ Seneca

Conflict cannot survive without your participation. ~ Wayne Dyer

Things could always be worse; for instance, you could be ugly and work in the Post Office. ~ Adrienne E. Gusoff

It's better to feed one cat than many mice. ~ Norwegian Proverb

"Few men have the natural strength to honor a friend's success without envy." ~ Aeschylus

If money does not bring happiness...Give me yours and be happy... Ha ha..!

When a man is artistic, it means that he is able to find a matching pair of socks.

A visitor comes with ten blessings, eats one, and leaves nine. ~ Kurdish Proverb

Treat people like they are the key to your success, because they may be. ~ Anonymous

You have succeeded in life when all you really want is only what you really need. — Vernon Howard

EVERYTHING in your life you have attracted. Accept that fact because it's true.

You move totally away from reality when you believe that there is a legitimate reason to suffer. ~ Byron Katie

Hold out your hands to feel the luxury of the sunbeams. — Helen Keller

Remember happiness doesn't depend upon who you are or what you have; it depends solely on what you think.

I've seen and met angels wearing the disguise of ordinary people living ordinary lives. ~ Tracy Chapman

You deserve to have whatever you truly want in your life.

Affirmation: I love who i am, I like where i am, I like where i've been & LOVE where Im Going.

"I am as my Creator made me and since He is satisfied, so am I". – Minnie Smith

Speak or act with an impure mind, And trouble will follow you. ~ Buddha

Maybe it's time I stop punishing myself and just allow myself to be happy?

"I hope you love birds too. It is economical. It saves going to heaven." ~ Emily Dickinson

Yoga is the cessation of the movements of the mind. Then there is abiding in the seer's own form. ~ Patanjali

Ulcers are caused not so much by what we eat as what's eating us.

The truth is: you don't HAVE a life, you ARE life. ~ Eckhart Tolle

It's good to leave each day behind, like flowing water, free of sadness. Yesterday is gone and its tale told. Today new seeds are growing. ~ Rumi

Every object, every being, is a jar full of delight. ~ Rumi

Chop your own wood, and it will warm you twice. ~ Henry Ford

One day our grandchildren will go to museums to see what poverty was like.

What we think about and thank about is what we bring about. – The Secret

God has put something noble and good into every heart His hand created.

There are no mistakes, no coincidences. All events are blessings given to us to learn from. – Elizabeth Kubler-Ross

Life is a blank piece of canvas and the world is the paint.

Circumstances and situations do color life but you have been given the mind to choose what the color shall be. ~ John Homer Miller

With every experience, you alone are painting your own canvas, thought by thought, choice by choice.

Our whole life is solving puzzles. ~ Erno Rubik

"Prayer is the answer, no matter what the question."

"Don't Call the World D I R T Y because you... FORGOT CLEAN YOUR GLASSES" ~ Aaron Hill

The Soul is here for its own joy. — Rumi

To experience peace – stop disturbing it! ~ TBFI

World peace or inner peace: Which is easier to achieve?

Love doesn't need to be perfect. It just needs to be true.

The thing that we call 'failure' is not the falling down, but the staying down ~ Mary Pickford

If you have a mom, there is nowhere you are likely to go where a prayer has not already been. ~ Robert Brault

Basic goodness is the foundation for extraordinary greatness.

Let your religion be less of a theory and more of a love affair ~ GK Chesterton

"The only real prison is fear, and the only real freedom is freedom from fear." ~ Aung San Suu Kyi

If you pull one pig by the tail all the rest squeak ~ Dutch saying

"Red sky at night, sailors delight; red sky at morning, sailors warning" ~ Proverb

If ur friend is too frank dat wat he/she says hurts u, Don't get mad 'Coz Donkey once told Shrek, "Only true friends can be cruelly honest."

Your parents may not always like you, but they will always love you.

In life, there is no room for blame, judgment, or criticism.

The reading of all good books is like a conversation with the finest minds of past centuries. ~ Rene Descartes

"When I count my blessings, I count you twice." ~ Irish Proverb

Hunger is the best sauce in the world. ~ Cervantes @FoodNuts

I asked God to give me happiness...God said "NO, I GIVE YOU BLESSINGS; HAPPINESS IS UP TO YOU...

People think I'm God... anywhere I go...they say "Oh God! You've come again..."

When I say 'I MISS SCHOOL' it means my 'FRIENDS AND THE FUN' not the 'SCHOOL'

I didn't want to pray to God 'cause I didn't want him to know where I was...

With our thoughts, we make our World ~ Buddha

You are the source of all that exists around you; you are the creator of your own world. ~ Osho

Stop being afraid of what could go wrong and think of what could go right!

Don't wait for someone else to make your life a happily ever after story. That's your job!

Forget past mistakes. Forget failures. Forget everything except what you're going to do now & do it. ~ William Durant

Of all the things you wear, your expression is the most important. ~ Janet Lane

Life is about always being appreciative of what you have and who you are.

All wrong-doing arises because of mind. If mind is transformed can wrong-doing remain? ~ Buddha

I think all humans suffer from an identity crisis at some point in their life: Makes me glad I'm a rabbit.

People, even more than things, have to be renewed, restored, revived, reclaimed, and redeemed. Never throw out anyone. ~ A.Hepburn

...never say: "what to love?" or "what to care?" because everyone around you are the people to love and care.

The world is disgracefully managed one hardly knows to whom to complain. ~ Ronald Firbank

"...we don't need laws, we need Morals!"

Every now and then it's good to pause in your pursuit of happiness and just be happy.

The present moment is a powerful goddess. ~ Goethe

Your big opportunity may be right where you are now!!!!!

"To discover joy is to return to a state of oneness with the Universe." ~ Peggy Jenkins

"Wake, butterfly — it's late, we've miles... to go together" ~ #haiku

"Do not fear thorns on your path; for they draw only corrupt blood. ~ Kahlil Gibran

"WE ONLY HAVE THIS MOMENT, Sparkling like a Star in our Hand... & M E L T I N G like a Snowflake" ~ Marie B. Ray

"I'm not smiling at you; I'm trying not to laugh."

"Perfect is boring, human is beautiful" ~ Tyra Banks

Children of the same mother do not always agree. ~ Nigerian Proverb

The intelligent want self-control; children want candy: I'm a child forever. ~ Rumi

Look deep into nature, and then you will understand everything better. – Albert Einstein

I think of life as a good book. The further you get into it, the more it begins to make sense. ~ Harold Kushner

Prayer is exhaling the spirit of man & inhaling the spirit of God.

"In meditation we turn off the channel of the world and switch on the channel of God." ~ Sant Rajinder Singh Ji

"When the eyes of the heart are opened, the creation is revealed as it really is…the body of Divine Light." ~ Andrew Harvey

Sometimes it's better to put love into hugs than to put it into words. ~ Unknown

Know that you ALWAYS have the answers, follow your intuition and your feelings.

Conversation enriches the understanding, but solitude is the school of genius. ~ Ralph Waldo Emerson

What are you fixing? What is broken? Truth is, there is nothing to fix but your own perception. ~*~ self

"Because, sometimes, some things are meant to stay broken"

JOY PEACE HAPPINESS…

A drop of ink may make a million think. ~ Proverb

Stop being afraid::: let life happen 2 u,, life is always in the right:: ALWAYS...

Progress is always a good feeling.

"Health best of all gains, and peace of mind is the best of all happiness." ~ The Mahabharata

"Every day in every way I am getting better and better and BETTER." #affirmation

Your mind is the compass that your body follows — point toward the positive direction.

Things never go so well that one should have no fear, and never so ill that one should have no hope. ~ Turkish Proverb

A mind that is fast is sick. A mind that is slow is sound. A mind that is still is divine. ~ Meher Baba

You use the mind nonstop – but when the mind quiets there is no more seeking for God. God finds you. ~ Sri Babaji

You are the honored guest. Do not weep like a beggar for pieces of the world. ~ RUMI

Even during your darkest night, the Sun within you remains intact and luminous. ~ Aleyah Hart

Relationship is not about perfection. It is about moments, feelings, and stories being shared.

In each of us is a little of all of us. ~ Georg Christoph Lichtenberg

Everyone is God speaking. Why not be polite and Listen? ~ Hafiz

God gave us two ears to hear, two eyes to see, and two hands to hold: But why only one heart? Because he wants us to find the other one

Every drop in the ocean counts. ~ Yoko Ono

I believe a leaf of grass is no less than the journey-work of the stars. ~Walt Whitman

Without God, our week: Mournday, Tearsday, Wasteday, Thirstday, Fightday, Shatterday and Sinday!

"Take everything as it comes, and tell your self that it is all coming from God." ~ Yogananda

God does notice us, and He watches over us but it is usually through another person that he meets our needs.

"Seeing myself in others and others in myself, whom could I harm, whom could I exploit?" ~ Buddha

You are "Life" itself, and not your "Life Situation". Instead of saying "I am sad", say "I have a feeling of sadness"

Just as a candle cannot burn without fire, men cannot live without a spiritual life. ~ Buddha

He who carries God in his heart bears heaven with him wherever he goes: ~ St. Ignatius

"You live more fully once you realise that the time spent being unhappy is wasteful." ~ Ruth E.Renki

Buddhist Prayer – May all beings everywhere plagued with sufferings of body and mind quickly be freed from their illnesses @Carla_is_love

All of us are creative. We will leave our mark on the world: Everyone in their own way.

Align with the stillness & be more mindful of what is to come rather than what was!

Not being known doesn't stop the truth from being true. ~ Richard Bach

There are many wonderful things that will never be done if you do not do them. ~ Charles D. Gill

When Confidence Grows- Anxiety Shrinks

Cheese and bread make the cheeks red. ~ German Proverb

"When someone rings the doorbell, why do dogs always assume it's for them?"

...do not insult the crocodile until you have crossed the river ~ Chinese proverb.

A little girl, asked where her home was, replied, "Where mother is." — Keith L. Brooks

We know nothing about motivation. All we can do is write books about it. – Peter F. Druckerj

Q: Why did the chicken say, Meow, oink, bow-wow, and moo? A: He was studying foreign languages.

No one appears on our stage unless the Director has placed them there for our benefit. ~ Paramahansa Yogananda

God writes the gospel not in the Bible alone, but on trees, & flowers, & clouds, & stars.

"Gratitude is when memory is stored in the heart & not in the mind." ~ Lionel Hampton

All the talents of God are within you. How could this be otherwise when your soul derived from His genes? ~ Hafiz

The words that enlighten the soul are more precious than jewels. ~ Hazrat Inayat Khan

Do all things lovingly. That is the secret to quality and excellence. ~ Gary Ryan Blair

Our dance is not with this or that; our dance is with the divine.

Thank you God for helping me to understand that this problem has already been solved for me.

Whisper a wish to a butterfly and it will fly up to heaven and make it come true.

You're not perfect, i'll tell you that. but i'll tell you something else.. you're beautiful.

In harmony with myself and others, with nature and all of life, I am happy and free.

All our answer's lie here: Listen to what the sea says: Ask the snowy mountains. @bkamatya

If you scramble about in search of inner peace, you will lose your inner peace. ~ Lao Tzu

God is the supreme shopkeeper; his market is infinite.

You were born on Earth to learn what Love is. This is your true purpose.

"Peace of mind means a quiet mind, not a noisy mind."

Life is inconvenient, unexpected, unplanned, unscripted, always messy, never on time; but oh-so-beautiful.

Life is/ profoundly/ mysterious./ Relax./ Let go./ Surrender into the mystery. ~ Leonard Jacobson

In the words of Arthur Dobin, let us all spell God with two O's.

Spiritual Healing is not just becoming free from pain; it is realizing that you were never really trapped. ~ James Keeley

Inner peace is always there; you merely have to seek and it will find you. ~ S A Jefferson

Allow yourself to be brand new today. The future is a blank canvas, don't paint your past there, paint a new scene!

"I searched for God and found only myself. I searched for myself and found only God". ~ Sufi Proverb

Go beyond your little world and find the grandeur of God's world. — Rumi

I don't pray really, because I don't want to bore God. ~ Orson Welles

Friendship is like a rainbow. Sharing 7 colors of feelings: love, sadness, happiness, truth, faith, secret, & respect

The road to a friend's house is never long. ~ Swedish proverb

"Why do you sit there looking like an envelope without any address on it?" ~ Mark Twain

"Everything is perfect in the universe – even your desire to improve it." ~ Wayne Dyer

The universe is a continuous web. Touch it at any point and the whole web quivers. ~ Stanley Kunitz

What if we simply loved & appreciated each other more?

I love you more today than yesterday but far less than tomorrow.

I've learned.... That having a child fall asleep in your arms is one of the most peaceful feelings in the world. @iHATEquotez

There's no point in being grown up if you can't be childish sometimes.

"Laughing is good EXERCISE. It's like jogging on the inside." ~ Unknown

"A mind at peace, a mind centered and not focused on harming others, is stronger than any physical force in the universe." ~ Wayne Dyer

The greatest man in history was the poorest. ~ Ralph Waldo Emerson

The chief function of the body is to carry the brain around. ~ Thomas Edison

When the trees sing to you, you know your yoga is working. ~ Denise Benitez

All the old separations between "holy" and "worldly" are not real. Everything is divine: Everything. ~ Mother Meera

Words, like nature, half reveal and half conceal the soul within. ~ Alfred Lord Tennyson

The greatest gift of the garden is the restoration of the five senses. ~ Hanna Rion

If you treat a sick child like an adult and a sick adult like a child, everything usually works out pretty well. ~ Black Hawk

When the cat and the mouse agree, the grocer is ruined. ~ Iranian Proverb

While physics & mathematics may tell us how the universe began, they are not much use in predicting human behavior /...

An aim in life is the only fortune worth finding. ~ Robert Louis Stevenson

Scientific truth may be put quite briefly; eat moderately, having an ordinary mixed diet, and don't worry. ~ Robert Hutchison

"I lived in that solitude which is painful in youth, but delicious in the years of maturity." ~ Albert Einstein

Lord, give me strength to make my precious people smile: I love them so much, my Family

Just because we don't speak the same way, doesn't mean we don't feel the same emotions.

Leadership is an opportunity to serve. It is not a trumpet call to self importance.

World is a THEATRE, Our life is a MOVIE, God is the DIRECTOR, Nature is the PRODUCER, U r the ACTOR...So perform WELL & enjoy the LIFE.

The most important question to ask about any work is "how does this serve the world?"- Marianne Williamson

We wish for you to know that you are powerful, you have nothing to fear. Do not doubt.

Happiness will never come to those who fail to appreciate what they already have. ~ Anonymous

"Don't wait for inspiration. It comes while one is working." ~ Henri Matisse

No-mind is realization No-mind is enlightenment. No-mind is liberation. ~ Osho

Do not speak, unless it improves on silence! – Buddhist Proverb

Whenever you go on a diet, try to avoid pink tablecloths or napkins. According to color studies, pink increases the appetite.

LIVELY NATURAL TRUE FEELINGS...

Your energy, your will, your God!

The woman gives birth to the son while the universe gave birth to the Sun. The woman is a smaller version of the bigger universe.

When you can't find peace outside yourself, find peace within yourself.

"The first rule of focus is... "Wherever you are be there" ~ Unknown

The circumference of life cannot be rightly drawn until the center is set. ~ Benjamin E. Mays

Despite the old saying, "Don't take ur troubles to bed" Many men still sleep with their wives!

Every thing is easy...when you are busy. Nothing is easy...when you are lazy. ~ Swami Vivekananda

Life is a constant struggle between right and wrong and good and evil, but do you know who always wins? ~ Fonzie

"Life is too deep for words, so don't try to describe it, just live it." ~ C.S. Lewis

Celebrate your existence by the life that you live.

I want to know who made this proverb: When poverty comes in at the door, love flies out of the window!!

He was a dreamer, a thinker, a speculative philosopher... or, as his wife would have it, an idiot. ~ Douglas Adams

Teacher: "How did you feel?" Monk: "Different." Teacher: "Different how?" Monk: "Well...for the first time, I felt really happy."

"I am as my Creator made me and since He is satisfied, so am I". ~ Minnie Smith

There is no loneliness to the clear-eyed mystic in this luminous, brimming playful world. ~ Hafiz

Wonder why people tell me to be quiet, when I'm loud but when I'm quiet, people ask me what's wrong with me.

The king is the man who can. ~ Thomas Carlyle

Whether we love once, twice, or a dozen times, we always face a brand-new situation. Love is always NEW ~ Paulo Coelho

The Universe is infinitely generous. There is more than enough for everyone.

Be like the flower; turn your faces to the sun! ~ Kahlil Gibran

~ The grace & truth of God to set you 'free' & help you 'be' are closer than you realize.

If you wish to embrace life, then embrace the globe. ~ Arnold Atlas

There are no such things as problems – only temporary situations without a solution.

Love me or leave me alone.

"Remember there's no such thing as a small act of kindness. Every act creates a ripple with no logical end." ~ Scott Adams

Love is sweet when it's new. But it is sweeter when it's true.

Be wise in the way you act toward others. Let your conversations always be full of grace.

Never go to a doctor whose office plants have died.

"Almost all of our unhappiness is the result of comparing ourselves to others."

Some people are so seasonal, admire you one day, reject you the next... Keep moving. ~ S.Whyte

There are many paths to God: I have chosen that of Music and Dancing. ~ Rumi

Get up a little earlier in the morning, so that you can spend more time with you.

Truth, like gold, is to be obtained not by its growth, but by washing away from it all that is not gold ~ Leo Tolstoy

I am a creation of God, an ever-renewing expression of divine life.

That was all a man needed: hope. It was lack of hope that discouraged a man. ~ Charles Bukowski

He who has a why to live can bear almost any how ~ Friedrich Nietzsche

"Voters don't decide issues; they decide who will decide issues." ~ George Will

Love is a state of being; it has nothing to do with anybody else. One is not in love, one is love ~ Osho

"I like long walks, especially when they are taken by people that annoy me." — Fred Allen

"If a little knowledge is dangerous, where is the man who has so much as to be out of danger?" — T.H. Huxley

If you have a particular faith or religion, that is good. But you can survive without it. ~ Dalai Lama

God says you are PERFECT, but the ego tells you are not. Who are you going to believe?

Yellow butterflies look like flowers flying through the warm summer air. ~ Andrea Willis

Dirt is not dirty, but only something in the wrong place. ~ Lord Palmerston

To keep the heart unwrinkled, to be hopeful, kindly, cheerful, and reverent–that is to triumph over old age.

If God were leaving u a text message, I think it would say: 'Enjoy yourself" ~ Marianne Williamson

Forgive yourself for doing things just for you.

"In the final analysis, it is between you and God. It was never between you and them anyway."

The eyes of others are our prisons, their thoughts our cages. ~ Virginia Woolf

Every moment of your life, including this one, is a fresh start. ~ Jean-Louis Servan-Schreiber

To send a letter is a good way to go somewhere without sending anything but your heart....Unknown.

Life is like a piano. The white keys r happiness, the black keys r sadness: Remember the black keys make music too.

When a child is born, so are grandmothers. — Judith Levy

I will act as if I do make a difference. ~ William James

The world is your reflection. Smile first if you'd like others to smile back at you.

Inside of You Is the Power to Be More Focused, Confident, Decisive, & Powerful!

The rose speaks of love silently, in a language known only to the heart. ~ Unknown

You make beautiful things. You make beautiful things out of the dust. You make beautiful things. You make beautiful things out of us.

Nothing has to be changed, because all is beautiful – that is enlightenment. ~ Osho

We need 4 hugs a day for survival. We need 8 hugs a day for maintenance. We need 12 hugs a day for growth. ~ Virginia Satir

When they first invented the clock how did they know what time to set it at??

Why is this thus? What is the reason for this thusness? ~ Artemus Ward

I used to be indecisive. Now I'm not sure.

As soon as your cart is turned over, everyone rushes to give you advice. – Russian Proverb

"Religion is belief in someone else's experience. Spirituality is having your own experience" ~ Deepak Chopra

Aim far, look far, you will go very far.

Everybody says they want to be free. Take the train off the tracks and it's free-but it can't go anywhere.

To stop drinking, study a drunkard while you are sober ~ Chinese proverb

"You Can Never When You Don't Ever." ~Jahangir

You think you're not pretty, someone is wishing to be as pretty as you. ..

Long life is the reward of the righteous; gray hair is a glorious crown. ~ Proverb

"When you see a good move, look for a better one" ~ Emmanuel Lasker (Chess champion).

All truth, in the long run, is only common sense clarified ~ Thomas Huxley

Water is composed of two gins. Oxygin and hydrogin. Oxygin is pure gin. Hydrogin is gin and water.

...i don't think you're an ugly person...you're a beautiful monkey. = D

Even the lion must defend himself against the flies. ~ German Proverb

Now is the time to know that all that you do is sacred. ~ Hafiz

...dear tummy, get ready because the food will attack now! xD HAHA!

If God only used perfect people nothing would ever get done. We are all trophies of God's grace.

Why worry when you can pray::: and why pray if ur gonna keep on worrying!!!

PLEASING INSPIRING!

Be a lamp, or a lifeboat, or a ladder. Help someone's soul heal. Walk out of your house like a shepherd ~ Rumi

Love, Harmony, Peace, Joy, Bliss, Light, Eternal, Creative, Wonderful, Beauty. It's You!

I'd rather love someone I can't have, than have someone I can't love. ~ Nick Jonas

At the start of 2010 I set out on a diet and aim to lose 30lbs. So far I've lost 10 months.

All men by nature desire knowledge!!! And women???

In Yoga I learned the definition of Namaste: The Divine in me acknowledges & sees the Divine in you.

Females don't cry because they're weak. It's because their love is too strong.

"The single most revolutionary thing you can do is recognize that you are enough" ~ Carlos Andrés Gómez

God, love, life and bliss all mean the same.

To Poet Philosopher Saint, all things are friendly and sacred, all events profitable, all days holy, all men divine. ~ Emerson

Your mind creates your heaven. Your mind can create the other 'h' word too.

Are you looking for profound experiences? Is the ordinary not extraordinary?

"Every friend is to the other a Sun, and a sunflower also. He attracts and follows."~ Jean Paul Richter

...it is what it is, it's not what it should have been, not what it could have been, it is what it is

Life is like a grammar lesson. You find the past perfect and the present tense.

It is not the fire in the fireplace which warms the house, but the couple who get along well. ~ Malagasy Proverb

You known you have grown up when ...You watch the weather channel.

Always keep the door open, so opportunity doesn't have to knock.

The hardest job kids face today is learning good manners without seeing any. ~ Fred Astaire

Everyone deserves to laugh. Everyone deserves to be happy. Everyone deserves to be loved.

"No one has ever loved anyone the way everyone wants to be loved." ~ Mignon McLaughlin

"After one look at this planet, any visitor from outer space would say, 'I want to see the manager.'" ~ William S. Burroughs

If men liked shopping, they'd call it research. ~ Cynthia

Buildings, too, are children of Earth and Sun. ~ Frank Lloyd Wright

// I write • in words • but the sun • writes poetry • in light // ~ #gogyohka

Never work. ~ Guy Debord

Some of God's greatest gifts are unanswered prayers. ~ Garth Brooks

Do not go in the direction of darkness – I tell you: suns exist. ~ Rumi

There is a battle that goes on between men and women. Many people call it love. ~ Edvard Munch

Mother is the first teacher. Teacher is the second mother.

What you dislike in another take care to correct in yourself. ~ Thomas Sprat

Venus is the only planet in our solar system which rotates in a clockwise direction. ~ N. Wylie Jones

"Let your head be more than a funnel to your stomach." German proverb

The soul that can speak with its eyes can also kiss with a gaze. ~ Unknown

"It is difficult to see the picture when you are inside of the frame." — Author Unknown

God gave us mouths that close and ears that don't – that should tell us something.

Teacher: "I told you to stand at the end of the line?" Little Johnny: "I tried, but there was someone already there!"

And there, in the midst of your life, is a more wonderful you than you could ever image. Begin to Believe in You!

I don't want the cheese; I just want out of the trap. ~ Spanish Proverb

Tomolo will never come, do it today.

Bank Manager asks Santa in an interview: What is Cyclone? Santa: It is the smallest Loan given by the Bank to purchase a cycle.

If you are not free to choose wrongly and irresponsibly, you are not free at all. ~ Jacob Hornberger

...i love my dad, i love my mom soooo much.. Family is sent from heaven. Simple truth, simple fact: D

Any man can lose his hat in a fairy wind. ~ Irish Proverb

"Impossible only means that you haven't found the solution yet." ~ Source Unknown

How glorious a greeting the sun gives the mountains! ~ John Muir

The most important moment of your life is – NOW! :)

"Good words help sick minds." ~ English proverb

Praise makes good men better and bad men worse. ~ English proverb

"Holy mother Earth, the trees & all nature, are witnesses of your thoughts & deeds." ~ Proverb

One leg in the past and one leg in the future leaves nothing to stand on for today. ~ Proverb

It's only in our minds that we are separate from the rest of the world. ~ Gay Luce

"Wait for Satisfaction and Your Wait Will be Satisfying." ~ Jahangir

All through nature, you will find the same law: First the need, then the means. ~ Robert Collier

"Good manners sometimes means simply putting up with other peoples bad manners"

If you cannot find the truth right where you are, where else do you expect to find it? ~ Dogen

I am free! I am blessed! I am prosperous! I am abundant! I am whole! I am joyful!

"Love and marriage, love and marriage, / Go together like a horse and carriage." Sammy Cahn song

Become a wisdom hunter, He who walks with the wise grows wise ~ Proverbs

Learning how to learn is life's most important skill. ~ Unknown

Love is giving, like saying "I love you the way you are," without prosecuting "Love me the way I am."

The breeze at dawn has secrets to tell you. Don't go back to sleep. ~ Rumi

What do you want? If it takes more than 2 sec to answer this you don't know.

We can let circumstances rule us or we can take charge & rule our lives from within. ~ Earl Nightengale

If there is a God, whence precede so many evils? If there is no God, whence cometh any good? ~ Boethius

He who knows nothing is closer to the truth than he whose mind is filled with falsehoods and errors. ~Thomas Jefferson

Today is a different day. You need to be a better person than yesterday.

"There is a reward for kindness to every living animal or human." ~ Prophet Mohammed

"Once a problem is solved, its simplicity is amazing". ~ Paulo Coelho

Calmness of mind is one of the beautiful jewels of wisdom.

PICK UP LINE: You must be a magician, because every time I look at you, everyone else disappears.

A beautiful life does not just happen; it is built daily by prayer, humility, sacrifice and love. ~ Dennis Castillo

Change is frightening. The past may have been miserable, but at least it was familiar.

After you've heard two eyewitness accounts of an auto accident, you begin to worry about history. ~ Unknown

With all your science – can you tell how it is, and whence it is, that light comes into the soul? ~ Thoreau

The best bridge between despair and hope is a good night's sleep. ~ E. Joseph Cossman

"You eat, in dreams, the custard of the day." Alexandar Pope

"Sometimes one smile means more than a dozen roses." ~ Anonymous

Do you like me as I am or should I ask God to improve your taste?

"Every second we live is a new and unique moment of the universe: A moment that will never be again." ~ Pablo Picasso

"Our beliefs about ourselves are the most telling factors in determining our level of success and happiness in life."

...someday u will find the one who will watch every sunrise with u until the sunset...

"Knowing how to count is wisdom!" ~ bro. eli soriano

I remember when the candle shop burned down. Everyone stood around singing "Happy Birthday"

"There must be more to life than having everything?" ~ Maurice Sendak

"For those who doubt, no miracle is sufficient." ~ Nancy Gibbs

Duty is God; Work is worship. Even tiniest work is a flower placed at the feet of God. ~ Sri Sathya Sai Baba

Make one person smile today...make it two...smile yourself.

Give yourself a break today. Let go of all self-criticism and allow joy to abound!

"Be aware of wonder, live a balanced life – Learn some, think some, play and work some every day." ~ Robert Fulghum

We are all prisoners but some of us are in cells with windows and some without. ~ #KahlilGibran

My whole approach towards life is that of total acceptance, is that of celebration, not of renunciation. ~ Osho

"The butterfly counts not months but moments, and has time enough" ~ Rabindranath Tagore

Just because I believe in God, it doesn't mean that I won't do bad, I'm just a human.

"Religion is regarded by the common people as true, by the wise as false, and by the rulers as useful." ~ Seneca

What is life? Look around you for a second. Life is what happens to you right now. That's life. ~ Philippos

The whole secret of a successful life is to find out what is one's destiny to do, and then do it ~ Henry Ford

If something's bound to happen, it will happen... Right time, right person, and for the best reason ~ Aristotle

Love is joy. Don't convince yourself that suffering is part of it. ~ Paulo Coelho

Gentleness in every kind of behavior: that is the praise of the wise man. ~ Egyptian Proverb

Whatever you do today; do it better tomorrow. ~ Robert Shuler

Let out a little more string on your kite. ~ Alan Cohen

We have to earn our wings every day. ~ Frank Borman

Always end the name of your child with a vowel, so that when you yell the name will carry. ~ Bill Cosby

Life may not always be as good as it should be, but it's never as bad as it could be!

"Just 'cause you got the monkey off your back doesn't mean the circus has left town." ~ George Carlin

"Learn to appreciate art," I told my girlfriend. She said, "How could I appreciate you, then?"

Good morning very beautiful Universe... thank you for your ever-present Love that joyfully cares for & nurtures all.

The president is not the most powerful person in the world; you are just as powerful.

Doing one thing at a time and doing it well is a form of physical meditation.

Keep your sense of proportion by regularly, preferably daily, visiting the natural world. ~ Catlin Matthews

Who am I in the midst of this thought traffic? ~ Rumi

You are here to enable the divine purpose of the universe to unfold. That is how important you are! ~ Tolle

"The miracle is not to fly in the air, or to walk on the water, but to walk on the earth." Chinese Proverb

"We are not here merely to make a living. We are here to enrich the world." ~ Woodrow Wilson

"Anyone can be an ACE: Attitude + Commitment = Excellence" Robert Inman

LIFE TRUTH WISDOM

"Positive thinking will let you do everything better than negative thinking will." ~ Zig Ziglar

Do not overestimate the competition and underestimate yourself. You are better than you think.
~ Tim Ferriss

"Books are dangerous. The best ones should be labeled "This could change your life."

I am not yet completely ignorant, for I do not know all the answers. ~ R Brault

"No day in which you learn something is a complete loss." ~ David Eddings

What good is it to envy the greener grass on the other side when there is so much to cherish in ones own weeds.

"Nature herself has imprinted on the minds of all the idea of God." ~ Cicero

The art of Loving is the art of looking at what is missing and seeing it complete...

Everyone and everything is doing its job perfectly – no mistake.

For single: Just because you're boyless / girlless doesn't mean you have to be joyless!

You can tell what a man is by what he does when he hasn't anything to do. ~ Anonymous

The basic paradox: everything is a mess, yet all is well. ~ Ezra Bayda

You were made by God and for God, and until you understand that, life will never make sense ~ Rick Warren

Forgive everyone, especially yourself, to gain your own happiness.

When I'm not in my right mind, my left mind gets pretty crowded.

Once the pin is pulled, Mr. Grenade is not our friend.

Feelings come in all colors.....paint a loving world with them.

"If you're going to be thinking anything, you might as well think big...." Try something new. ..

Peter was a simple fisherman, yet God qualified him for the job by the power of the Holy Spirit.

I am perfect as I am. Put that thought in your heart for the day and see what happens.

Suffering is the result of insisting that something be other than it is. ~ Ezra Bayda

I wanna have a son before I have a daughter so my son can hurt anyone who hurts my little girl.

No God, no peace. Know God, know peace. ~ Unknown

Life is a teaching movie customized specially and perfectly for you.

So you want to become my son-in-law." "Not exactly: I just want to marry your daughter."

There is nothing as remarkable as learning how to think better ~ Unknown

"The most manifest sign of wisdom is continued cheerfulness." ~ Michel de Montaigne

So, I love you because the entire universe conspired to help me find you. ~ #Alchemist

"Every child born into the world is a new thought of God, an ever fresh and radiant possibility" ~ Kate Douglas Wiggin

Not all bad habits are unproductive.

Because our body is limited and our mind is unlimited, that's why we need a way to connect them. #yoga

"One forgives to the degree that one loves" ~ Francois de La Rochefoucauld

Love doesn't need to be perfect, it just need to be true.

Swallow grief and swallow anger but feed others with sweetness.

The activist is not the man who says the river is dirty. The activist is the man who cleans up the river. ~ Ross Perot

You are the perfect you and you're doing the best that you can in this moment. ~ Keith leon

Thank you, God, for the good things and the bad. Experiencing the bad helps us to appreciate the good.

if life worth living? that depends on the liver — Unknown

"People always emphasize the negative – no one puts up a sign: Beware – nice dog." —Unknown

How can there be a winner if someone loses? ~ Gandhi

My love is perfect even though I am not.

"The best things in life are unexpected – because there were no expectations." ~ Eli Khamarov

"Success is about enjoying what you have and where you are, while pursuing achievable goals." ~ Bo Bennett

"Your true nature is purity, peace, and joy." ~ Sai Baba

"Joy is very infectious; therefore, be always full of joy." ~ mother Theresa

"Beauty is being in harmony with what you are." ~ Peter Nivio Zarlenga

"Within you there is a stillness and a sanctuary to which you can retreat at any time and be yourself." ~ Hermann Hesse

"The elderly are the Books of the Young" ~ Bedouin proverb

You go from village to village on your horse asking everyone- "Has anyone seen my horse?" ~ Rumi

"I don't ask anybody to follow any particular path. I just tell them to be what they are, in their natural state," ~ Nisargadatta

"If your life is full of darkness, ask God for a candle."

One girl of junior school wrote – The seven wonders are: to touch taste see hear feel laugh and to love. Enjoy your gifts!

The family is one of nature's masterpieces. ~ George Santayana

The family with an old person in it possesses a jewel. ~ Chinese saying

Children have become so expensive that only the poor can afford them. ~ Anonymous

The mind is the source of happiness and unhappiness. ~ Buddha

Love: Two minds without a single thought.

A cat knows exactly what you are, and treats you accordingly.

"Better to be filled with wonder than to be filled with doubt" ~ Unknown

Good friends are good for your health. ~ Irwin Sarason

"I don't hate people, I just feel better when they aren't around" ~ Charles Bukowski

Who is rich? He that is content: Who is that? Nobody ~ Benjamin Franklin

"You have your way. I have my way. As for the right way, the correct way, & the only way, it does not exist." ~ Nietzsche

"As you breathe in cherish yourself. As you breathe out cherish all beings" ~ Dalai Lama

"Let the waters settle, you will see stars and moon mirrored in your being." ~ Rumi

Exercise is king, nutrition is queen and together you have the entire kingdom!" ~ Jack Lalanne

"A leader takes people where they want to go? ~ Rosalynn Carter

"Any book you open will benefit your mind." ~ Chinese Proverb

"I need to know that it's possible that two people can stay happy together forever." ~ Juno

"To be closer to God be closer to people" ~ Kahlil Gibran

Let your child know "The world is a safe place!"

If you wouldn't write it and sign it, don't say it. ~ Earl Wilson

If thou are a master, be sometimes blind; if a servant, sometimes deaf. ~ Thomas Fuller

Events and circumstances may change – but wherever you go – there you are! ~ Cheryl Janecky

"I'd like to be so rich that my dog has a dog"

"Incidents, Accidents and Happenings are Natural: Natural Is Super Natural?"

"Philosophy is a study that lets us be unhappy more intelligently" ~ Unknown

Keep your tents separate and bring your hearts together. ~ Arab proverb

A good day for me begins with knowing, whether I feel like it or not, my life and work have purpose.

Men are what their mothers made them. ~ Ralph Waldo Emerson

The Parents Sacrifice: "If there must be trouble let it be in my day, that my child may have peace" ~ Thomas Paine

PEACEFUL SELF!

"Be yourself! I mean, who else is really qualified to do it??~"

"Some people care too much, I think its called love"~ Winnie the Pooh

You can spend minutes, hours, days, weeks or even months over-analyzing a situation... or u can just leave the pieces & move on! ~ Tupac

"A man chases a woman... until she catches him." ~ American Proverb

A perfection of means, and confusion of aims, seems to be our main problem. ~ Einstein

People travel to faraway places to watch, in fascination, the kind of people they ignore at home. ~ Runes

The major problems in the world are the result of the difference between how nature works and the way people think. ~ G.Bateson

It is more difficult to contend with oneself than with the world. ~ Turkish Proverb

My luck is so bad that if I bought a cemetery, people would stop dying. ~ Rodney Dangerfield

If you want pretty nurse, you must be patient. ~ Proverb

You need not aspire for or get any new state. Get rid of your present thoughts, that is all ~ Ramana Maharshi

"Assert your right to make a few mistakes. If people can't accept your imperfections, that's their fault." ~ Dr. David M. Burns

"When angry, count ten before you speak; if very angry, a hundred." ~ Thomas Jefferson

A smart husband buys his wife very fine china so she won't trust him to wash it.

"Miracles are not contrary to nature, but only contrary to what we know about nature." ~ Saint Augustine of Hippo

Irony in life – a man who can carry a 100kg rice sack load on his back cannot buy it.

In the eyes of a child, there are 7 million wonders of the world. @Quotes2U

The imagination of nature is far, far greater than the imagination of man. ~ Richard Feynman

Have you ever felt scared, left out, sad, angry, shocked, hurt, alone or worthless? Congratulations, you're a normal person.

"When diet is wrong medicine is of no use. When diet is correct medicine is of no need." ~ Ayurvedic Proverb

Go often to the house of thy friend; for weeds soon choke up the unused path. ~ Proverb

"Every time I see your face, I realize that God really does have a sense of humor."

"Don't wait for the perfect moment, take the moment and make it perfect." ~ Unknown

"When you shoot an arrow of truth, dip its point in honey." ~ Arab Proverb

Heaven means to be one with God. ~ Confucius

When you teach your son, you teach your son's son. ~ The Talmud

God is everywhere but He is most manifest in man. So serve man as God. That is as good as worshiping God. ~ Ramakrishna

You are joy. We are all the different kinds of laughing.

The entire world is a laboratory to the inquiring mind. ~ Martin Fischer

When the sun rises & finds someone still sleeping, she thinks he/she is dead; Get up!

TRUTH WE SEEK!

Have no doubt ... your inner wisdom will always guide you.

Life was never meant to be a struggle. It is meant to be joyous, loving, and enjoyable.

So simple, so rare: "Successful people believe things CAN be done."

"No man becomes rich unless he enriches others." ~ Andrew Carnegie

"Men are at war with each other because each man is at war with himself." ~ Francis Meehan

"The ideas that have lighted my way have been kindness, beauty and truth." ~ Albert Einstein

I am not a teacher, but an awakener. ~ Robert Frost

It's practically impossible to look at a penguin and feel angry. ~ JOE MOORE

The most important of life's battles is the one we fight daily in the silent chambers of the soul. ~ David O. McKay

"I vow to let go of all worries and anxiety in order to be light and free." ~Thich Nhat Hanh

Nobodies perfect except people who can draw a circle perfectly.

Life's Little Instruction Book: Keep an extra key hidden somewhere on your car, in case you lock yourself out!

The most certain sign of wisdom is cheerfulness. ~ Montaigne

Children are all foreigners. ~ Ralph Waldo Emerson

If we knew what it was we were doing, it would not be called research, would it? ~ Einstein

Don't let the noise of others' opinions drown out your own inner voice. ~ Steve Jobs

Air is nourishment and requires time to be digested, just like any liquid or solid food: Breath slowly, deeply and with awareness.

...my African proverb for class: NO SWEET W/O SWEAT!

To fear is one thing. To let fear grab you by the tail and swing you around is another. ~ Katherine Paterson

Being a philosopher, I have a problem for every solution.

"What a wonderful life I have had! I only wish I'd realized it sooner". ~ Colette

Know that you ALWAYS have the answers, follow your intuition and your feelings.

When I quote others I do so in order to express my own ideas more clearly. ~ Michel de Montaigne

"The cyclone derives its powers from a calm center. So does a person." ~ Norman Vincent Peale

Isn't everything we do in life a way to be loved a little more?

"Nothing exists except atoms and empty space; everything else is opinion." ~ Democritus

Keep your heart in wonder!

"Don't approach a goat from the front, a horse from the back, or a fool from any side." ~ Yiddish proverb

The cat was created when the lion sneezed. ~ Arabian Proverb

INTERESTING THOUGHTFUL

Promise yourself to live your life as a revolution and not just a process of evolution. ~ Anthony J. D'Angelo

Bananas are the world's most popular fruit after tomatoes:

A library is thought in cold storage. ~ Herbert Samuel

Just because I want some milk sometimes, it doesn't mean I have to buy a cow. ~ Unknown

Daily Affirmations: My inner quest is rewarding and provides me with all the answers I need.

A clear conscience laughs at false accusations.

"If your prayer is fulfilled, be thankful. If it is not, still be thankful. That is the beauty of prayer." ~ Osho

Always depend upon the calm knowledge you can be master of anything that may happen to you. ~ Norman Vincent Peale

God created a perfect world of imperfect living beings which are constantly evolving towards perfection.

Don't miss out on a blessing because it isn't packaged the way you expect.

Each relationship, business venture, job, & phase of our lives, serve as platforms for us to grow...

If it walks like a duck, quacks like a duck, looks like a duck, it must be a duck ~ Proverb

Don't wait for the Last Judgment. It happens every day. ~ Albert Camus

The names of the cards in the deck (Ace, two, three ...Jack, Queen, King) add up to 52 letters #coolfacts

We only do three things in life: we sit, we stand, we lie horizontal: The rest is just a story.

"Hope is the only bee that makes honey without flowers." ~ Robert Green Ingersoll

I got a simple rule about everybody. If you don't treat me right — shame on you! – Louis Armstrong

Seek justice for others without personal gain for oneself and you will learn to do good...

To drink is human. To drink coffee is DIVINE. ~ Gloria Jeans

What is the purpose of life? "To be the eyes and ears and conscience of the Creator of the Universe, you fool". ~ Kilgore Trout's

To err is human. To blame it on someone else is even more human. #murphyslaws

PEARLS OF WISDOM!

...you're lucky to love something that loves you!

The most beautiful clothes that can dress a woman are the arms of the man she loves. ~ Yves Saint Laurent

God turns u from one feeling to another & teaches u by means of opposites, so that u will have two wings to fly...

Gratitude is a powerful process for shifting your energy and bringing more of what you want into your life.

There're 3 words I like 2 repeat 2 myself: glass half full, Just 2 remind myself 2 b grateful 4 everything I ha

The words of the world want to make sentences.

Within the problem lies the solution!! ~ Milton Katselas

A woman's heart should be so lost in God that a man needs to seek Him in order to find her.

Cheerfulness is the best promoter of health and is as friendly to the mind as to the body. ~ Joseph Addison

All problems of existence are essentially problems of harmony: ~ Sri Aurobindo

Breathing is a miracle. Seeing is a miracle. Tasting is a miracle. Thinking is a miracle. YOU are a miracle. LIFE is a miracle.

A computer once beat me at chess, but it was no match for me at kick boxing.

I've got to keep breathing: Because tomorrow, the sun will rise. Who knows what the tide could bring? ~ Castaway

Put all excuses aside and remember this: YOU are capable. ~ Zig Ziglar

Jewish Proverb ~ Truth is the safest lie.

Looking for a better place? Wherever you go – there you are! You take yourself with you. ~ Cheryl Janecky

I am thankful for all my life experiences.

If you reveal your secrets to the wind, you should not blame the wind for revealing them to the trees.

School Doctor: Have you ever had trouble with appendicitis? Fred: Only when I tried to spell it.

Redneck Vocabulary: Cheer – A piece of furniture used for sitting.

Mostly men show how they really feel about you without words: Pay attention to their actions.

It's simple to be wise. Just think of something stupid to say, & then don't say it.

I wish love is like baby shampoo: Because it has "no more tears" formula.

Happiness: a good bank account, a good cook and a good digestion. ~ Rousseau, Jean Jacques

The guy who invented the first wheel was an idiot. The guy who invented the other three, he was the genius.

You weren't born because of the mistakes. God has chosen you when planning creation.

Forgive and give are two powerful words because they can make people around you smile.

God doesn't want something from us. He simply wants us. ~ C.S. Lewis

Thanks God for this beautiful life: I don't know about your plans, but I must face all of them with all my heart.

Every baby born into the world is a finer one than the last. ~ Unknown

I don't want pray to be a rich person. But I want pray to be a useful person for others or at least for myself.

There is nothing wrong in America that can't be fixed with what is right in America. ~ William J Clinton

FEEL

YOU=CHOCOLATE. Always make me feel better.

A simple way 4 "HAPPY LIVING" is just to forget 2 things in LIFE. (1) The GOOD u did for others. (2) The BAD done by others to u.

"We can change our lives. We can do, have, and be exactly what we wish." ~ Tony Robbins

If you desire to be pure, have firm faith without wasting your energy in useless scriptural discussions and arguments. ~ Ramakrishna

A friend is someone who lets you have total freedom to be yourself

Funny: Never ask a barber if he thinks you need a haircut.

We are connected to the rest of the Universe

Mental health is the process of trading one set of problems for a more interesting set of problems. ~ Nathaniel Brandon

"When you tell a lie, you steal someone's right to the truth." ~ The Kite Runner

Dysfunctional family: any family with more than 1 person in it. ~ Mary Karr

Can we love ourselves enough to unconditionally love the energy we are? ~ Dee Wallace

"Remain open. There is something bigger than you know going on here."– Iyanla VanZant

"Not all of us have to possess earthshaking talent, just common sense and love will do."– Myrtle Auvil

There is no surprise more magical than the surprise of being loved. It is God's finger on man's shoulder ~ Charles Morgan

"We shall never know all the good that a simple smile can do…" ~ Mother Teresa

Be a breath of fresh air to ALL who inhale you!

Life itself is the most wonderful fairy tale ~ Hans Christian Andersen

When we sigh about our problem, they grow D_O_U_B_L_E, but when we laugh about them they become o o o o o bubbles!

We are...the Reflection of all we have seen, all we have felt, and those we have loved...

Two eyes see more than one. – Portuguese Proverb

LIVE LOVE LIFE!

If it makes you happy it can't be that bad.

The man who speaks the truth is always at ease. ~ Persian proverb

There is no limit to how happy you can be.

Let life happen to you. Believe me; life is in the right, always.

If you want the truth, ask a child.

Our solar system consists of one star and some debris.

When did I realize I was God? Well, I was praying and I suddenly realized I was talking to myself.

When I read about the evils of drinking, I gave up reading.

You can't make someone love you. All you can do is be someone who can be loved, and the rest is up to them.

Don't let a week go by without telling someone that you love them.

A fish and a bird can fall in love, but where will they live – Japanese proverb

For some strange reason, no matter where I go, the place is always called "here". — Ashleigh Brilliant

"If this is coffee, please bring me some tea; if this is tea, please bring me some coffee." – Abraham Lincoln

Our days are happier when we give people a bit of our heart rather than a piece of our mind.

Inner beauty will always win out over outer beauty in the long run. ~ Michelle Medina

Most people live unbalanced lives because they have too much knowledge and not enough wisdom.

I am lying in bed unable to turn off the chatter of my monkey mind… ~ Baba Ram Dass

Love is the light that dissolves all walls between souls, families & nations: ~ Yogananda

Realize that each person has limitless abilities, but each of us is different in our own way.

There is more wisdom in your body than in your deepest philosophies. ~ Friedrich Nietzsche

"A rose given during life is better than orchids on the grave". ~ Anon

I propose that we make mosquitoes our National Insect. Then the government will protect them and they will become extinct.

"Life is a precious gift. Don't waste it being unhappy, dissatisfied, or anything else you can be." ~ Unknown

God is always willing to help you. He never leaves you no matter how bad you are.

What should you do if you see an endangered animal eating an endangered plant?

Every child born into the world is a new thought of God, an ever-fresh and radiant possibility. ~ Kate Douglas Wiggin

"Find ecstasy in life; the mere sense of living is joy enough." – Emily Dickinson

"Enlightenment is but recognition, not a change at all." ~ Unknown

I miss the way we USED to be: When everything's fine, everything's alright and everything's okay.

Happiness consists of three things: Someone to love, work to do and a clear conscience.

Man makes holy what he believes, as he makes beautiful what he loves. — Ernest Renan

It is more important to do the right thing than to do the thing right – Drucker

Peace is your natural state. It is the mind that obstructs the natural state. ~ Ramana Maharshi

"Trust means trusting that where so much beauty is being showered, the source of such beauty must exist." ~ Osho

A sad soul can kill you quicker than a germ. — John Steinbeck

The bicycle is a curious vehicle. Its passenger is its engine. ~ John Howard

"One of the most important things you should strive for in life is peace of mind..."

The reason angels can fly is because they take themselves lightly. ~ G.K. Chesterton

Those who are awake live in a state of constant amazement. ~ Buddha

You love simply because you cannot help it. – Kim Anderson

Lips only smiles are half joys, lips + eyes smiling = FULL JOYS.

"Happiness is easy, but learning not to be unhappy, can be difficult". ~ Dr. Wayne Dyer

Common sense is what tells us the Earth is flat and the Sun goes around it. ~ Anon

Those who are really Rich "need nothing". Yoga/God consciousness = the state of needing nothing.

My grandma walks like a Penguin and when I think about it she's also shaped like one.

NICE WISE...

Always walk through life as if you have something new to learn and you will. ~ Vernon Howard

What we see depends mainly on what we look for. ~ Sir John Lubbock

Every now and then it's okay to color outside the lines.... Think outside the box... Be Change!

Seen on the back of a biker's vest: If you can read this, my wife fell off...

"The wave does not need to die to become water. She is already water." ~ Thich Nhat Hanh

♫ well there's three versions of this story ♫ mine, yours and then the truth ♫

"Twitter was invented by a man. A woman would have chose a higher character limit"

I am a magnet attracting love, health, happiness, wisdom, and wealth from the universe. I am so grateful.

God doesn't require us to succeed; he only requires that you try. ~ Mother Teresa

Homer Simpson: If you really want something in life you have to work for it. Now quiet, they're about to announce the lottery n...

God gives, gives, gives & forgives. People get, get, get & forget.

The thousand mysteries around us would not trouble but interest us, if only we had cheerful, healthy hearts. ~ Friedrich Nietzsche

"Here is a great way of dealing with the burdens of life: Accept that some days you're the pigeon, and some days you're the statue."

The universe as we know it is a joint product of the observer and the observed" ~ Chardin

Computer is made of bits, man is made of habits.

There is not enough darkness in the whole world to put out the light of a single candle. ~ Anonymous

The glass is neither half-full nor half-empty: it's twice as big as it needs to be. ~ Unknown

Opportunities do not come with their values stamped upon them. ~ Maltbie Babcock

What is always speaking silently is the body. ~ Norman Brown

Every breath is an opportunity to receive and let go. I receive love and I let go of pain. ~ Brenda MacIntyre

A good friend understands you even when your thoughts aren't fitting into words.

Her love is Heaven on Earth!

When walking through the 'valley of shadows', remember, a shadow is cast by a light. ~ H.K Barclay

#offensivecompliments Girl 1- ooo looks u put on a few pounds. Girl 2 - ooo great we can start wearing eachother clothes!!!

You don't choose your family. They are God's gift to you, as you are to them. ~ Desmond Tutu

Notice the signs of grace throughout the day. The universe is communicating with you.

I am alone in nothing. Everything I think or say or do touches all the universe... ~ A Course in Miracles

Helped a blind lady cross the road; she had very soft hands.

Is there any other way to see the world than from within?

"Men should learn to live with the same seriousness with which children play" ~ Nietzsche

Art is collaboration between God and the artist, and the less the artist does the better. ~ Andre Gide

What is a free gift? Aren't all gifts free?

There are no losers in a world where we all share the same energy source. ~ Wayne Dyer

This is the reason we cannot complain of life it keeps no one against his will. ~ Seneca

A critic can only review the book he has read, not the one which the writer wrote. ~ Mignon McLaughlin

"Any kid who has two parents interested in him and has a houseful of books isn't poor" – Sam Levinson

INTERESTING INSPIRING...

The true miracle is not walking on water or walking in air, but simply walking on this earth. ~ Thich Nhat Hanh

Untrustworthy: a person whose stomach never moves when he laughs.

"Where there is joy there is creation. Where there is no joy there is no creation: know the nature of joy." ~ Upanishads

We awaken in others the same attitude of mind we hold toward them. ~ Elbert Hubbard

I'm feeling a little sensitive today so be nice or I'll cry ~_~

God will forgive me. It's his job. ~ Heinrich Heine

There is no 'i' in team, but there is in win.

I'm a little fish in a big pond but I still make a splash

When I was young, I admired clever people. Now that I am old, I admire kind people. ~ Abraham Joshua Heschel

Make a wish, it might come true.

I'm on a seafood diet. I see food and I eat it. ~ Author Unknown

Give neither advice nor salt, until you are asked for it. – English Proverb

Not the senses I have but what I do with them is my kingdom. ~ Helen Keller

We are always in the forge, or on the anvil; by trials God is shaping us for higher things. ~ Henry Ward Beecher

Have you ever seen a cow with a mobile phone? It has come to my attention that cattle prefer to live off the GRID!

That's the secret to life... replace one worry with another... ~ Charles M. Schulz

...dear mom: you're a queen. you deserve the cream. everything that gleam. everything that shines. everything that's mine

Remember that, "generous people are rarely mentally ill people" – Dr Karl Menninger

A patriot must always be ready to defend his country against his government. ~ Edward Abbey

The real menace in dealing with a five-year-old is that in no time at all you begin to sound like five-year-old. ~ Joan Kerr

A jack of both sides is before long, trusted by nobody, and abused by both parties. ~ Proverb

"He too serves a certain purpose, who only stands and cheers" ~ H. B. Adams

My fake plants died because I did not pretend to water them...

Rolfe Neill ~ Reading transports me. I can go anywhere and never leave my chair. It lets me shake hands with new ideas.

When I am right nobody remembers: When I am wrong nobody forgets!

I search for the warm atmosphere and smile.

The cow is nothing but a machine which makes grass fit for us people to eat. – John McNulty

Love is an act of endless forgiveness, a tender look which becomes a habit. ~ Peter Ustinov

A single lie that was discovered is enough to create a contagious doubt over every other truth expressed.

Solitude is impractical and yet society is fatal. ~ Emerson

He loved the rain. She came into his life and gave him an umbrella.

Reality is always kinder than the stories we tell about it. – Byron Katie

"Nature and Books belong to the eyes that see them." ~ Ralph Waldo Emerson

"Keep steadily before you the fact that all true success depends at last upon yourself." – Theodore T. Hunger

Man is the only creature that refuses to be what he is. ~ Albert Camus

"If you are happy when you are alone, you have learned the secret of being happy. Now, you can be happy together." – Osho

CHEERFULNESS

"Cheerfulness and contentment are great beautifiers and are famous preservers of youthful looks." ~ Charles Dickens

"I would rather have a mind opened by wonder than one closed by belief." ~ Spence

It's just you and your thoughts, which you have the power to change at every moment of every day. ~ Mabel Katz

See what is good, strong & beautiful in those around you!

#notetoteachers education should teach us how to think, rather than what to think!

Let everything be exactly as it is. Take a breath and let it go. Can we let it be this simple? ~ Cheri Huber

Don't try to be different. Just be good. To be good is different enough. ~ Arthur Freed

In the book #TheAlchemist the philosophy of life echoes "I'm an adventurer, looking for treasure."

Think about how lucky you are to actually be alive. What a miracle.

Temper your view of the world, let go of negative feelings. ~ Ann Tran

There is no power or dominion in heaven or upon earth that can separate you from the love of God.

Noise proves nothing. Often a hen who has merely laid an egg cackles as if she laid an asteroid. ~ Mark Twain

My doctor said, "You're out of shape." I said, "What are you talking about, Doctor, round is a shape!"

I've learned that under everyone's hard shell, is someone who wants to be appreciated and loved. ~ Andy Rooney

"I wish people would grow hearts instead of ego." ~ Unknown

Two men look out the same prison bars; one sees mud and the other stars. ~ Frederick Langbridge

"A puppy plays with every pup he meets, but an old dog has few associates." ~ Josh Billings

"As you simplify your life, the laws of the universe will be simpler." ~ Henry David Thoreau

How do you stop a thundering herd of Apes? Hold up your arm and say 'Go back, you didn't say 'May I?'

If you let restlessness move you, you lose touch with who you are: ~ Lao Tzu

Everything alive is sacred; life delights in life. ~ William Blake

Freedom from the desire for an answer is essential to the understanding of a problem. – Jiddu Krishnamurti

B4 u criticize some1, walk a mile in their shoes. That way ur a mile away and u have their shoes

The true measure of success is how much joy you feel on a regular basis!

Customer: Do you serve lobsters? Waiter: Yes sir, we serve anybody! ~ Charles Grave

#youknowwhatsannoying bitter people who are, in fact, bitter for no real reason

The cow is nothing but a machine which makes grass fit for us people to eat. — John McNulty

Heaven has a road, but no one travels it. Hell has no gate but men will dig 2 get there. – Chinese Proverb

The church is near but the road is icy; the bar is far away but I will walk carefully. — Russian Proverb

"The cobra will bite you whether you call it cobra or Mr. Cobra." ~ Proverb

Always hold your head up, but be careful to keep your nose at a friendly level. — Max L. Forman

"Flowers are a proud assertion that a ray of beauty out values all the utilities of the world." ~ Ralph Waldo Emerson

I don't know if God exists, but it would be better for His reputation if He didn't. – Jules Renard

More gold has been mined from the thoughts of men than has been taken from the earth. – Napoleon Hill

This life force is you. You are the mystery. You are the journey. You are exquisite. You are here. Now, it's your time.

Happiness is variable, depending on circumstances; Joy is constant, regardless of circumstances.

No matter what you going through, Remember God is using you. For the battle is not yours...It's the Lord's.

Men are from earth. Women are from earth. Deal with it.

AMAZING

#Ilikeyoubecause you resemble what God says a man should be.

Be a student of life. Learn something new every day.

You are swimming in the miracle all the time — you just don't see it. ~Jeff Foster

...life is not hard; it only needs some positive thinking

Charles Dickens ~ It was the best of times it was the worst of times.

Whenever i can't find something it just magically appears when my mom looks

Chance is a word void of sense; nothing can exist without a cause. ~ Voltaire

"I have never met a man so ignorant that I couldn't learn something from him." – Galileo Galilei

Friends are red, friends are blue, friends are yellow, friends are white: Friendship is COLORFUL!

The only abnormality is the incapacity to love. – Anais Nin

"The house does not rest upon the ground, but upon a woman". ~ Mexican Proverb

Born to make you happy, then who will make me happy?

The weather-cock on the church spire would soon be broken if it did not understand the art of turning to every wind. – Heinrich

Beautiful things I have seen so far: 1) a perfect grey sky 2) fox cub 3) flock of doves rising from a field 4) raven 5) a cabbage white butterfly

Listen to inspiring mentors - read inspiring books. Put good thoughts into your brain.

U weren't put on this earth to complain. U are here to change the things u're complaining about.

She cried and softly said, "He may be an old man, but he's my old man!" There wasn't a dry eye in the ICU when my mother left. #love

If you are a gardener of love, you will plant a smile on the faces of all you meet, for bringing beauty is your duty.

Never desert your own line of talent. Be what nature intended you for, and you will succeed ~ Sydney Smith

Brain cells come and brain cells go, but fat cells live forever!

Teacher: What time do you get up in the morning? About an hour and a half after I arrived at school

The same sun that melts butter hardens clay.

MAN NATURE GOD

The human spirit needs to accomplish, to achieve, to triumph to be happy. ~ Ben Stein

The world is your school. ~ Martin H. Fischer

"Your strength is in how calmly, quietly and peacefully you face life."

Cheerfulness is what greases the axles of the world. Don't go through life creaking. ~ H.W. Byles

My childhood may be over, but that doesn't mean playtime is. ~ Ron Olson

"You will always be your child's favorite toy" – Vicki Lansky

Humility is not thinking less of yourself, but thinking of yourself less – C.S.Lewis

If nothing ever sticks to TEFLON, how do they make TEFLON stick to the pan?

How do you know the perfect path for you? The one that is effortless and filled with joy!

It is the woman who chooses the man who will "choose" her.

My boss is so unpopular even his own shadow refuses to follow him.

Two goldfish in a bowl talking: Goldfish 1: Do you believe in God? Goldfish 2: Of course, I do! Who do you think changes the water?

Only a mother names her blind child, "Padmalocan" (lotus eyes). ~ Proverb

Life is a gift. Never forget to enjoy and bask in every moment you are in. ~ unknown

Judge: Where will you go if you tell a lie? Criminal: To hell. J: And where will you go if you speak the truth? C: To jail!

When you say "don't look" everyone looks, but if you say "look" no one looks.

To love is Forgiving because to love is For-Giving.

See God in every person, place, and thing, and all will be well in your world. ~ Louise Hay

"Modern technology Owes ecology An apology." ~ Alan M

Whenever there is a hard job to be done I assign it to a lazy man; he is sure to find an easy way of doing it.

What is the biggest lie ever? "I have read and agree to the terms of use"

The world is neutral. The way you approach it, the way you make use of it, makes you happy or unhappy. ~ SwSatchidananda

If Heaven made him – earth can find some use for him. ~ Chinese Proverb

"The end result of wisdom is... good deeds." ~ The Talmud

A wise man and a fool together, know more than a wise man alone. ~ Italian Proverb

God in His infinite wisdom Did not make me very wise- So when my actions are stupid They hardly take God by surprise. ~ L. Hughes

It is the mind that makes one wise or ignorant, bound or emancipated." ~ Sri Ramakrishna

Human errors can only be avoided if one can avoid the use of humans. ~ David L. Parnas

GREAT

"You have everything you need for complete peace and total happiness right now." ~ Wayne Dyer

Happiness is not the absence of problems but the ability 2 deal with life constructively & lovingly.

Be kind, for everyone you meet is fighting a hard battle. ~ Plato

"Look for the good in every person and every situation. You'll almost always find it." ~ Brian Tracy

Every smile makes you a day younger. ~ Chinese Proverb

I have no enemies, No! I have friends who don't understand me.

Self-Realization is effortless. What you are trying to find is what you already are. ~ Ramesh Balsekar

And I just want a place in society. Is that too much to ask for??

The universe is a continuous work of infinite genius, ever creative, ever merciful and ever in love with you.

"Your strength is in how calmly, quietly and peacefully you face life."

Cheerfulness is what greases the axles of the world. Don't go through life creaking. ~ H.W. Byles

My childhood may be over, but that doesn't mean playtime is. ~ Ron Olson

A diet of positive thoughts detoxifies the mind and improves your quality of life. ~ Margaret Stockley

"I am a little pencil in the hand of a writing God who is sending a love letter to the world." ~ Mother Teresa

"..May your pockets hold always a coin or two" #irish #blessing

The basic paradox: everything is a mess, yet all is well. ~ Ezra Bayda

"No matter where you go or what you do, you live your entire life within the confines of your head." ~ Terry Josephson

"No duty is more urgent than that of returning thanks." ~ James Allen

"When the mouse laughs at the cat, there is a hole nearby." ~ Nigerian Proverb

Movement is a medicine for creating change in a person's physical, emotional, and mental states.

Surrender into the Oneness of All That Is, surrender into the acknowledgment that is so deeply within you.

When you stop being afraid, you feel good. ~ Spencer Johnson

When people feel valued & important something inside of them shifts & things begin to change.

The usefulness of a cup is in its emptiness. ~ Old Chinese Proverb

When you realize your potential to feel good, you will ask no one to be different in order for you to feel good.

The highest revelation is that God is in every man. ~ Emerson

Man is harder than rock and more fragile than an egg. ~ Yugoslav Proverb

"Respect for one's parents is the highest duty of civil life." – Proverb

#therewasatimewhen "log on" meant throwing more wood in the fire…

We need to shut down the chatter of the world to hear God within. ~ Rajinder Singh

Spiritual wealth is available to all regardless of outer circumstances. ~ Rajinder Singh

Nothing ever becomes real till it is experienced — even a proverb is no proverb to you till your life has illustrated it. — John Keats

Laughter on one's lips is a sign that the person down deep has a pretty good grasp of life. ~ Hugh Sidey

It is not what we eat but what we digest that makes us strong. ~ Francis Bacon

For shiny moisturized nails put 1 drop of baby oil onto each nail bed.

"A little Consideration, a little Thought for Others, makes all the difference."

Remember to count your blessings. I have counted all of you. Thank you friends...

If God had wanted me otherwise, He would have created me otherwise. ~ Johann von Goethe

Success is not the key to happiness. Happiness is the key to success. Love what u do & u shall be successful. ~ Buddha

You can't push anyone up the ladder unless he's willing to climb. ~ Louise

#ismilewhen when I go outside and see the beautiful green scenery that God has put on this earth...

"A realized sage abides in perfection; he has no need at all to gain anything." ~ Sri Nisargadatta Maharaj.

That one is learned who has reduced his learning to practice. ~ Proverb

"She likes you, you like her, why do you have to make it so complicated?" (about movies novels life) ~ Hannah Montana

"No shade tree? Blame not the sun, but yourself." ~ Chinese Proverb

"Fear can keep us up all night long, but faith makes one fine pillow."

"Focus 90% of your time on solutions and only 10% of your time on problems." ~ Anthony D'Angelo

"Every inch of space is part of the infinite living universe." ~ Veronica Ray

"Many of us crucify ourselves between two thieves – regret for the past and fear of the future." ~ Fulton Oursler

Saying yes to life means saying yes to everything, even longing, fear and pain. ~ Ezra Bayda

"So far the only successful substitute for brains is silence." ~ Anonymous

Be proud of the Amazing Soul You Are! Love Yourself. I Love You!

QUOTES! PROVERBS! SAYINGS!

Life is a quest not a question, a mystery not a problem. ~ Osho

"I am convinced that life is 10% what happens to me and 96% how I react to it."

"When you find peace within yourself, you become the kind of person who can live at peace with others."

Be an explorer. The universe is filled with wonder and magical things. ~ Flavia

"Microsoft Word will never understand that my name is NOT a spelling mistake."

Make yourself an honest man, and then you may be sure there is one less rascal in the world. ~ Thomas Carlyle

It is not time that changes man, nor knowledge; the only thing that can change someone's mind is love. ~ Paulo Coelho

"As a child I noticed adults looking so stressed, disconnected, fake & humorless compared to me & my friends & vowed 2 never become like them."

"Life is good, except when it's not....and even then it still is!"

"You cannot rid yourself of negative thinking, it is a human characteristic: Unless you are superhuman."

The person who can bring the spirit of laughter into a room is indeed blessed. ~ Bennett Cerf

"Heaven isn't a place... it's a FEELING!"

"Look for the beauty around you: Little things, big things, wondrous things, every thing!"

It needs no effort to be ecstatic; it needs great effort to be miserable: Ecstasy is our very nature. ~ Osho

"God is beyond comprehension, yet his love is so real."

When you pray, don't give God instructions... Just report for duty!

Are you on here all the time looking for "god"? Go outside and look at the sky, maybe a tree. It's a term that means Nature.

The whole existence is a temple...the trees are continuously in worship, the clouds are in prayer and the mountains are in meditation. ~ OSHO

Without freedom from the past, there is no freedom at all, because the mind is never new, fresh, and innocent. ~ J. Krishnamurti

"You create more drama in your life by the thoughts you choose to think."

Let us be grateful to the mirror for revealing to us our appearance only. ~ Samuel Butler

"Every man alone is sincere. At the entrance of a second person, hypocrisy begins."

"Give me real talk and I'll give u real respect."

You are the sculptor of your life experiences. Your Picasso is your Mind! ~ Lesetz

No dreamer is ever too small; no dream is ever too big.

The best and most efficient pharmacy is within your own system. ~ Robert C. Peale

Natural sunshine for vitamin D as well! >> "Kangaroo": mother care better than any incubators.

Our own life is the instrument with which we experiment with the truth. ~ Thich Nhat Hanh

Only the spoon knows what is stirring in the pot. ~ Sicilian Proverb

When dealing with people, remember you are dealing with creatures of emotion. ~ Dale Carnegie

Always kiss your children goodnight – even if they're already asleep. ~ H. Jackson Brown

...that's my sister's father ~ african american proverb

"The most important thing in communication is to hear what isn't being said."

"Each FLOWER is a Soul... ~B L O S S O M I N G~ Out to Nature" ~ Gerard De Nerval

Wake at dawn with a winged heart and give thanks for another day of loving. ~ Khalil Gibran

The best time to do something significant is between yesterday and tomorrow. ~ Zig Ziglar

A pile of rocks ceases to be a rock when somebody contemplates it with the idea of a cathedral in mind. ~ Antoine De Saint

"A B C D E F G H I J K L M N O P Q R S T V W X Y Z ... Did i miss any thing ? no.. I kept 'U' in my heart."

Pick up Line: Boy: Hey...is your name Google? Girl: No. Boy: but you have all the things I'm searching for...!

"She fell in love at second sight. When she first met him she didn't know how rich he was."

"Even though a marriage is made in heaven, the maintenance work has to be done here on earth."

"Marriage is when a man and woman become as one; the trouble starts when they try to decide which one."

"It's hard to choose a way when a heart and mind say something so much different."

"Your head must bow to your heart."

"Life isn't perfect, but it does have perfect moments."

Let go! Don't try to struggle, don't make life a conflict. Enjoy it! ~ Osho

We do not have to visit a madhouse to find disordered minds; our planet is the mental institution of the universe. ~ Johann von Goethe

People from a planet without flowers would think we must be mad with joy the whole time to have such... ~ Iris Murdoch

"Help thy brother's boat across, and lo! thine own has reached the shore!"

"Joy is what happens when we allow ourselves to recognize how good things really are."

"When I see your face, there's not a thing that I would change because you're amazing, just the way you are!"

"Trust that your life is unfolding perfectly, exactly as it should be."

To love someone is to see a miracle invisible to others. ~ Francois Mauriac

"He isn't perfect nor me. Our feelings aren't perfect. Our lives aren't perfect. But we love each other."

The most important question in the world is, 'Why is the child crying' ~ Alice Walker

Where there is room in the heart there is always room in the house… ~ Moore

Keep a green tree in your heart & perhaps a singing bird will come. ~ Chinese Proverb

"The only person who always got his work done by Friday was Robinson Crusoe."

"Let all living beings be free from disease and mental worries."

"I greet every person with a silent wish that great joy be in their life."

The universe rejoices whenever a kind word is spoken. ~ Philip Arnold

The kindest thing you can do for the people you care about is to become a happy, joyous person. ~ Brian Tracy

Learn to get in touch with the silence within yourself and know that everything in this life has a purpose. ~ Elizabeth Kubler-Ross

"Some minds are like concrete thoroughly mixed up and permanently set."

To love someone means to see him as God intended him. ~ Fyodor Dostoyevsky

"Our perfection is beyond blame or judgment. We are unconditionally perfect."

May you have warmth in your igloo, oil in your lamp, and peace in your heart? ~ Eskimo proverb

"There is no one like you. The mould was broken when God made you. You are a one-of-a-kind."

Do not be too timid and squeamish about your actions. All life is an experiment. ~ Ralph Waldo Emerson

Live the life you love. Love the life you live. ~ Bob Marley

The meaning of life is whatever you ascribe it to be. Being alive is the meaning. ~ Joseph Campbell

Love is what we were born with. Fear is what we learned here. ~ Marianne Williamson

I no longer seek good fortune I AM good fortune. ~ Walt Whitman

Your future depends on many things, but mostly on you. ~ Frank Tyger

"To get to heaven, turn right and keep straight."

Life is a shipwreck: But let's sing in the lifeboats. ~ Voltaire

Keep in mind that everyone's heart comes with an invisible "Fragile – Handle with Care" label.

"Tired of overcomplicated situations: Tired of emotions: Someone give me a robot heart."

Some people are not meant for you to love, but meant for you to learn. ~ Renee Vivian

I had three chairs in my house; one for solitude, two for friendship, three for society. ~ Henry David Thoreau

A hundred men may make an encampment, but it takes a woman to make a home. ~ Chinese Proverb

One must ask children and birds how cherries and strawberries taste. ~ Johann von Goethe

They are happiest who have power to gather wisdom from a flower. ~ Mary Howitt

There are no passengers on Spaceship Earth: Everybody's crew. ~ Marshall McLuhan

We sit together the mountain and I, until only the mountain remains. ~ Li Po

They are never alone that are accompanied with noble thoughts. ~ Sir Philip Sidney

To live long and achieve happiness, cultivate the art of radiating happiness. ~ Malcolm Forbes

"Don't regret what might have been. Accept what is and rejoice in what is yet to be..."

Do not search for the truth. Only cease to cherish opinions. ~ Seng T'San

Your task is not to seek love, but to merely seek and find all the barriers within yourself that you have built against love. ~ Rumi

Muddy water, let stand becomes clear. ~ Lao Tzu

Let life happen to u. Believe me: life is in the right, always. ~ Rainer Maria Rilke

"Let's eat Grandma! Let's eat, Grandma! Punctuation saves lives."

Position of a husband is like a split AC. No matter how loud it's outside, but inside the house, it's designed to remain silent!

"My wife is such a bad cook, in my house we pray after we eat."

"I wish the dogs could differentiate between intruders and the cat. I'm not happy about their enthusiasm at 2am."

Dogs laugh, but they laugh with their tails. ~ Max Eastman

Seriousness is a sickness; your sense of humor makes you more human... ~ Osho

"I'd love to go out with you, but the man on television told me to say tuned."

"Consciousness is always present and therefore our fundamental nature is always present. We are pure wakefulness."

For attractive lips, speak words of kindness. For lovely eyes, seek out the good in people. ~ Audrey Hepburn

Is solace anywhere more comforting than in the arms of a sister? ~ Alice Walker

A wise son brings joy to his father, but a foolish son grief to his mother. ~ Proverb

Today, and every day, give thanks for your teachers, and your teachers' teachers.

Let food be thy medicine, thy medicine shall be thy food. ~ Hippocrates

When the solution is simple, God is answering. ~ Albert Einstein

"Be urself. It doesn't matter what other's think. Speak truth. This will change the world."

There is no loneliness to the clear-eyed mystic in this luminous, brimming playful world. ~ Hafiz

There is not one blade of grass; there is no color in this world that is not intended to make us rejoice. ~ John Calvin

Wrestling with God always and inevitably has a positive outcome. We become freer from within. ~ Janina Gomes

"Meditation is better than Medication"

It doesn't matter who you love, or how you love, but that you love. ~ Robert Browning

Reflection is looking in so you can look out with a broader, bigger & more accurate perspective. ~ Mick Ukleja

You are not just a drop in the ocean; you are mighty ocean in the drop. ~ Rumi

Zoo: An excellent place to study the habits of human beings. ~ Evan Esar

Words can sting like anything, but silence breaks the heart. ~ Phyllis McGinley

Be a rainbow in someone else's cloud. ~ Maya Angelou

"You are not what you think you are, but what you think, you are"

. . . Rivers and mountains, plants and animals, the sun, the moon and the stars, you and I all are expressions of this one Reality. ~ Amma

From there to here, and here to there, funny things are everywhere. ~ Dr. Seuss

Instead of saying "God I have a big problem," say "Problem I have a BIG God." ~ S.Whyte

"When you enJOY something, you bring the spirit of JOY to the activity."

God made Truth with many doors to welcome every believer who knocks on them. ~ Kahlil Gibran

"The world's a playground. You know that when you're a kid, but somewhere along the line everybody forgets it."

"Children really brighten up a household – they never turn the lights off."

The universe has a way of timing things for your benefit. ~ Aine

"The birds are singing to me this morning and they all seem to be saying the same thing: It's a beautiful day to be happy."

In every living thing there is the desire for love. ~ D.H. Lawrence

"The more closely aligned we are to our true, divine nature, the holier each experience becomes."

"You speak to God when you pray...God speaks to you when you meditate."

God is really only another artist. He invented the giraffe, the elephant and the cat. He has no real style. ~ Pablo Picasso

"I have yet to see a perfect car, a perfect laptop, a perfect house, but i am lucky that all the roses i get are perfect."

To the question of your life you are the answer, and to the problems of your life you are the solution. ~ Joe Cordare

Hold up your hands before your eyes. You are looking at the hands of God. ~ Rabbi Lawrence Kushner

A house is a home when it shelters the body and comforts the soul. ~ Phillip Moffitt

Of all the things you wear, your expression is the most important. ~ Janet Lane

Be patient with everyone, but above all with yourself. ~ St. Francis de Sales

Kindness makes a fellow feel good whether it's being done to him or by him. ~ Clark Frank

Terrified Female screams: "What are you, why do you chase me, what will you do to me?" Monster: "How should I know, it's your dream."

The greatest virtues are those which are most useful to other persons. ~ Aristotle

The first sign of maturity is the discovery that the volume knob also turns to the left. ~ Jerry M Wright

The guy who discovered milk....What was he doing with that cow? ~ Louise

Dear Math, Grow up and solve your own problems... ~ Louise

Trust yourself. You know more than you think you do. ~ Benjamin Spock

"Syazar, Pazar, Shwozar " (Simplicity, Truth, Purity) said Bhagwan Gopinath, a Kashmiri sage.

"It is a joy to know that all that I am seeking finally is none other than the Infinite Peaceful & Joyful witness that I already Am!"

"All is a perfect dance of Wholeness."

There is always a way to do it better... find it! ~ Thomas A. Edison

A man is the sum of his actions, of what he has done, of what he can do. Nothing else! ~ Mahatma Gandhi.

Travel light, live light, spread the light, be the light. ~ Yogi Bhajan

Never feel lonely. You are never lonely. At the deepest core of your being, God resides. ~ OSHO.

"The world when seen through a little child's eyes greatly resembles paradise."

"Trust that the universe has the most beautiful life aligned for you right now."

This is the time. This is the place. This is the vastness. Right here is paradise. Always: Always. ~ Byron Katie

There's always a work in progress – be it in the mind, the soul, the heart, or in your hands. ~ Rick Howse.

"Look at the people in your life today, go past the notion you have of them, and see how magnificent they truly are."

Feeling gratitude and not expressing it is like wrapping a present and not giving it. ~ William Arthur Ward

"Acknowledge that every moment in your life is a true blessing."

"Every day may not be good, but there's something good in every day."

There is no shortage of good days. It is good lives that are hard to come by. ~ Annie Dillard

Love the moment & the energy of that moment will spread beyond all boundaries. ~ Corita Kent

He, who wants to change his past, must change his present. ~ Eugene Williams

"Don't envy for what people have and you don't. You have something they don't have."

Life is a festival only to the wise. ~ Ralph Waldo Emerson

Do not be too timid or squeamish about your actions. All Life is an Experiment. ~ Ralph Waldo Emerson

Happiness is essentially a state of going somewhere, wholeheartedly, one-directionally, without regret or reservation. ~ William H. Sheldon

"I know... one word acceptance another tolerance yet another peace."

Number one is the loneliest number. ~ Eugene williams

"All of life is spiritual, and therefore all of life's problems are spiritually based – and spiritually solved."

Every one of us is a wonder. Every one of us has a story. ~ Kristin Hunter

Who in the world do you think you are? A Superstar? Well right you are! ~ John Lennon

The truest greatness lies in being kind, the truest wisdom in a happy mind. ~ Ella Wheeler Wilcox

Life is not a problem to be solved, nor a question to be answered. Life is a mystery to be experienced. ~ Alan Watts

In this life we cannot always do great things. But we can do small things with great love. ~ Mother Teresa

Do not neglect to show hospitality to strangers, for by this some have entertained angels without knowing it. ~ Hebrews

I don't eat junk food and I don't think junk thoughts. ~ Peace Pilgrim

Rivers know this: there is no hurry. We shall get there some day. ~ Winnie the Pooh

A line is a dot that went for a walk. ~ Paul Klee

"More doors R opened with "please" than with keys."

"Ever since the ice age, people seem to be in quest for a divine union and enlightenment."

Nobody's family can hang out the sign: Nothing the matter here. ~ Chinese proverb

"I've no reason to laugh, but when I looked around I had no reason to cry."

We are the leaves of one branch, the drops of one sea, and the flowers of one garden. ~ Lacordaire

"You are searching Truth, all are searching Truth; Aim is same, need not be any reason of discord!"

Don't burn the flag; wash it. ~ Norman Thomas

The ornament of a house is the friends who frequent it. ~ Ralph Waldo Emerson

It is very difficult to find a parent who is satisfied. Not even the father of Buddha was satisfied. ~ Osho

Things will get better-despite our efforts to improve them. ~ Will Rogers

People of humor are always in some degree people of genius. ~ Samuel Taylor

"City Birds sing at higher pitch 2 compete with noise."

You just have to trust that life has a road mapped out for you. ~ Orlando Bloom

"God created you to show off His beauty!"

Know the true nature of your Beloved. In His loving eyes your every thought, word and movement is always beautiful. ~ Hafiz

There are three truths: my truth, your truth and the truth. ~ Chinese Proverb

I like the silent church before the service begins, better than any preaching. ~ Ralph Waldo Emerson

People have one thing in common: they are all different. ~ Robert Zend

If life were easy, then it would be boring. ~ Charles Beck

If it takes a lot of words to say what you have in mind, give it more thought. ~ Dennis Roch

"Being loved, and knowing that they are loved, makes people confident, relaxed and happy

What do we live for, if it is not to make life less difficult for each other? ~ GE

"Mind is enlightened: Self is light."

"There is always, always, always something to be thankful for."

The love of one's country is a splendid thing. But why should love stop at the border? ~ Pablo Casals

I don't know what weapons will be used in world war three, but in world war four people will use sticks and stones. ~ Albert Einstein

I said to the almond tree, "Friend, speak to me of God," and the almond tree blossomed. ~ Nikos Kazantzakis

"What is love? In math, it's a problem. In history, it's a battle. In science, it's a reaction. In art, it's a heart."

"There will always be a 'lie' in be"lie"ve, an 'over' in 'lover' an "end" in fri"end"s, "us" in tr"us"t and an "if" in l"if"e."

"Loving one another is not about forgetting our differences; it is about celebrating them…"

A human being's first responsibility is to shake hands with himself. ~ Henry Winkler

"Ego is disconnection with existence. By operating from ego one is against the wholeness."

It is possible for a man to see the forms of God, or to think of Him as a Person, only as long as he is conscious that he is a devotee. From the standpoint of discrimination this 'ego of a devotee' keeps him a little away from God. ~ Sri Ramakrishna

I believe God is managing affairs & He doesn't need any advice from me. ~ Henry Ford

When the mind is perfectly clear, "what is" is what we want. ~ Byron Katie

"The only miracle you need is the miracle happening now." ~ Unknown

Nothing is separate; like waves in the ocean, everything is interconnected: You are never alone. ~ Osho

Stop talking, stop thinking, and there is nothing you will not understand. ~ Kanchi Sosan

If you can watch your breath for 60 minutes, without a moment's destruction, you are already enlightened. ~ Buddha

Let there be nothing within thee that is not very beautiful and very gentle. ~ James Allen

"The teacher you need is the person you're living with." ~ Unknown

No happening affects your real being – this is the absolute truth. ~ Nisargadatta

WORTH PONDERING

AMAZING WONDERFUL – IT'S LIFE...

Inner wealth is wisdom. Those who are rich in the inner world are those who have abundant wisdom ~ Ryuho Okawa

Have a good day, count your blessings, and pass this along to remind everyone else how blessed we all are. ~ R. Gordon

...parents: your room is a mess me: you should see my life...

...my childhood is ruined! Mom: OMG :(

...i have so much homework ... □□ □□ ...which movie should i watch?

Rabbits jump and they live for 8 years. Dogs run and they live for 15 years. Turtles do nothing & they live for 150 years. Lesson learned

Teacher: "Where were you born?" Student: "New York, Sir." Teacher: "Which part?" Student: "All of me, Sir."

Me: I'm too full to eat anymore. Food: Are you sure. Me: No.

Chocolate is made of cocoa which is made from plants. Therefore chocolate = salad

Me opening the fridge: "Baby you light up my world like nobody else."

Nobody's a natural. You work hard to get good and then work to get better.

Learn to be patient. If you don't, your impatience will make a patient out of you sooner or later. — Philip Arnold

Wishing things were different is a great way to torture yourself.

You are so beautiful that you give the sun a reason to shine.

We are all blessed to have the things we do have.

God understands our prayers even when we can't find the words to say them.

Negative thoughts create negative beliefs which govern our attitudes and actions to create negative results: GUESS WHAT POSITIVE THOUGHTS DO?

We are all part of the same being equal in every way ~ Speaking Tree

Man's spirituality and being are perfect.

Truth is revealed. It needs only to be practiced. ~ Mary Baker Eddy

Let us strive to reach a state in which we are able to see all beings on earth as a part of our own Self. ~ Amma @WEPromote

Receive grace, give grace. God wants what He gives us to flow through us to others.

Only beauty can see beauty. When you appreciate something beautiful, know that it is a reflection of you.

Yoga is said to be the oneness of breath, mind, and senses.

Yoga has a sly, clever way of short circuiting the mental patterns that cause anxiety. ~ Baxter Bell

We are never either so wretched or so happy as we say we are ~ Honor de Balzac

We must try to contribute joy to the world. That is true no matter what our circumstances. We must try. ~ Roger Ebert

You're not perfect, my friend. No one is. But you're precious to God.

Whenever you get pressured and tired, just say, "God never created this beautiful creation to be stressed."

Printed in Great Britain
by Amazon

83059170R00061